OMNIBEASTS

animal poems and paintings by

Douglas Florian

harcourt, inc.

ORLANDO • AUSTIN • NEW YORK • SAN DIEGO • TORONTO • LONDON

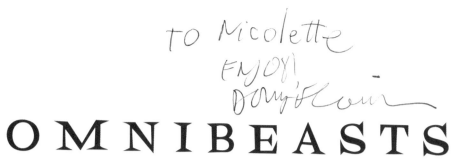

OMNIBEASTS

www.HarcourtBooks.com

The Chihuahua, The Persian, The Cheetah, The Ocelot, and The Jaguarundi
from *bow wow meow meow* copyright © 2003 by Douglas Florian

The Skink, The Python, The Polliwogs, The Glass Frog,
The Newt, The Bullfrog, and The Spring Peepers
from *lizards, frogs, and polliwogs* copyright © 2001 by Douglas Florian

The Bactrian Camel, The Fox, The Coyote, The Mule,
The Boar, The Porcupine, and The Tiger
from *mammalabilia* copyright © 2000 by Douglas Florian

The Daddy Longlegs, The Army Ants, The Praying Mantis,
The Monarch Butterfly, The Crickets, and The Mayfly
from *insectlopedia* copyright © 1998 by Douglas Florian

The Salmon, The Starfish, The Flounders, The Blenny, The Clam, and The Tetra
from *in the swim* copyright © 1997 by Douglas Florian

The Egret, The Vulture, The Roadrunner, The Hawk,
The Woodpeckers, and The Nightjar
from *on the wing* copyright © 1996 by Douglas Florian

The Walrus, The Anteater, The Armadillo, The Caterpillar, The Toad,
The Bat, and The Kangaroo
from *beast feast* copyright © 1994 by Douglas Florian

Library of Congress Cataloging-in-Publication Data
Florian, Douglas.
omnibeasts: animal poems and paintings/by Douglas Florian.
p.   cm.
1. Animals—Juvenile poetry. 2. Children's poetry, American.
[1. Animals—Poetry. 2. American poetry.] I. Title.
PS3556.L589O46 2004
811'.54—dc22   2003018823
ISBN 0-15-205038-8

First edition
A C E G H F D B

MANUFACTURED IN CHINA

For Jack, Jacob, Dora, and Esther

Contents

The Fox

Clever.
Cunning.
Crafty.
Sly.
A fox composed this poem,
Not I.

The Jaguarundi

The jaguarundi hunts by day
    Then sleeps inside its lair.
And when it wakes it likes to play
    In jaguarundi-wear.

The Skink

Along the ground I'm found—I slink.
Through grass I pass—I am a skink.
Bite my tail and it releases.
I don't fight back—
I *fall* *to* *pieces.*

13

The Army Ants

Left

        Right

Left

        Right

We're army ants.

We swarm.

    We fight.

We have no home.

We roam.

We race.

You're lucky if

We miss your place.

The Anteater

The
   anteater's
        long
            and
               tacky
                  tongue
                      is
                         snaking
                             from
                                its
                                   snout.

A thousand termites riding in,
But no one riding out.

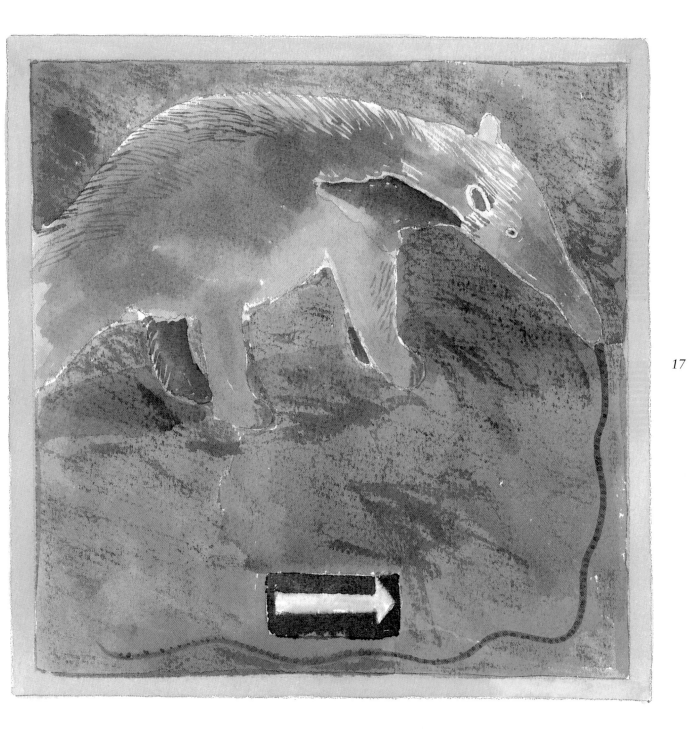

The Blenny

There are uglier fish than a blenny—

But not many.

The Armadillo

The armadillo
As a pillow
Would really be swell
Except
For the fact
That it comes in a shell.

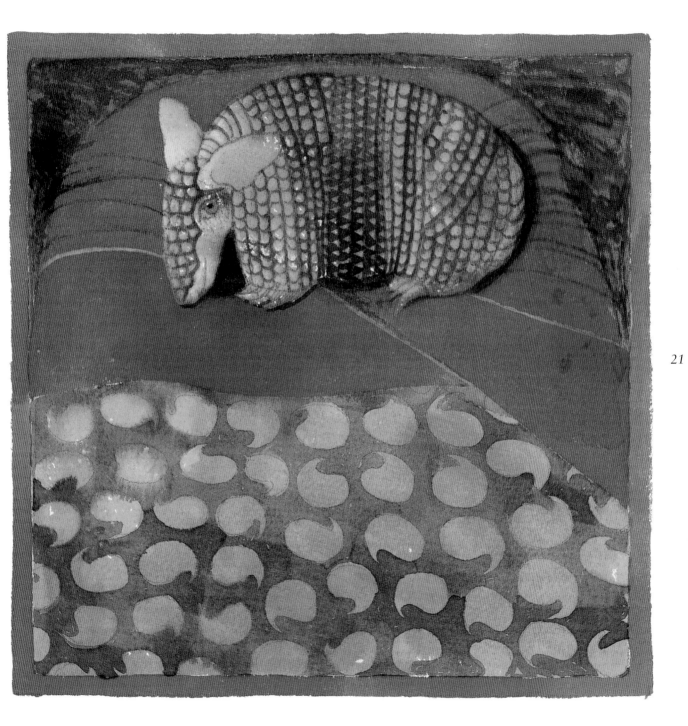

The Tiger

I am a cat—come hear me purrrr.
I've many stripes upon my furrrr.
I speed through forests like a blurrrr.
I hunt at night—I am tigerrrr.

The Polliwogs

We polliwoggle.
We polliwiggle.
We shake in lakes,
Make wakes,
And wriggle.
We quiver,
We shiver,
We jiggle,
We jog.
We're yearning
To turn ourselves
Into a frog.

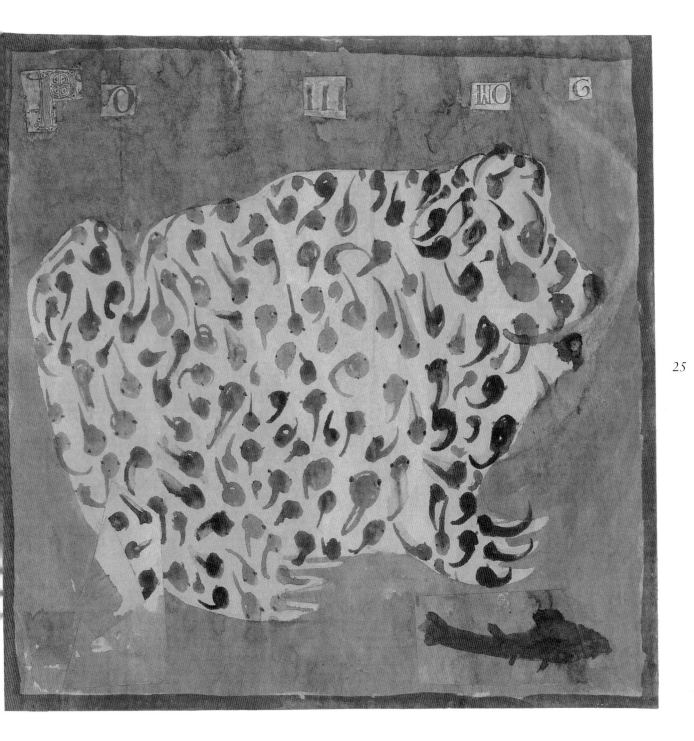

The Clam

They say, "As happy as a clam,"
But would *you* like to have to cram
Your body deep inside a shell?
And furthermore: I think clams smell.

The Bactrian Camel

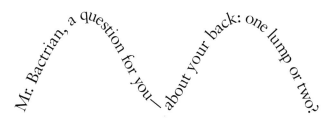

Mr. Bactrian, a question for you— about your back: one lump or two?

The Egret

On morning tide
An egret sat
And gave the beach
A feathered hat.

The Bat

The bat is batty as can be.
It sleeps all day in cave or tree,
And when the sun sets in the sky,
It rises from its rest to fly.
All night this mobile mammal mugs
A myriad of flying bugs.
And after its night out on the town,
The batty bat sleeps

Upside down.

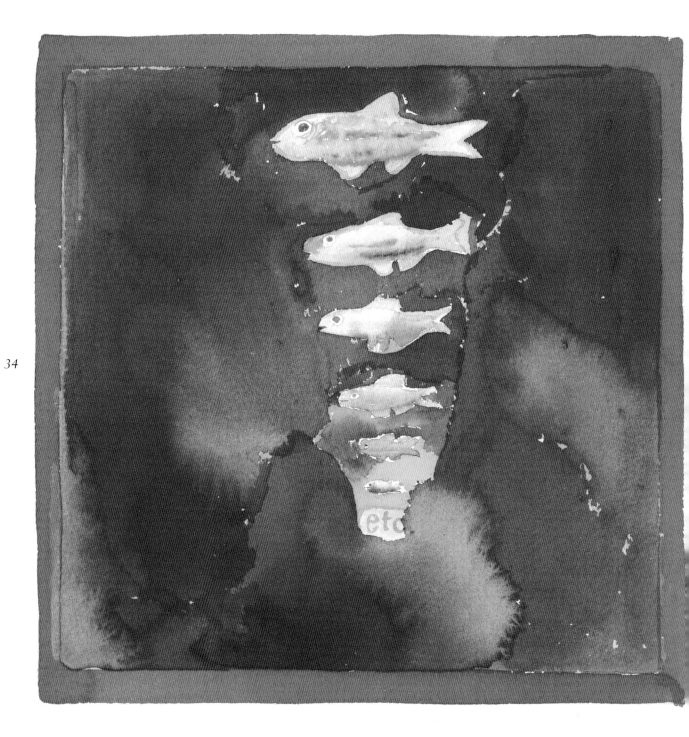

The Tetra

The itty-bitty, pretty tetra
Is small, minute, petite, et cetra.

The Vulture

Two things I know about the vulture:
Its beak
        is strong.
It's weak
        on culture.

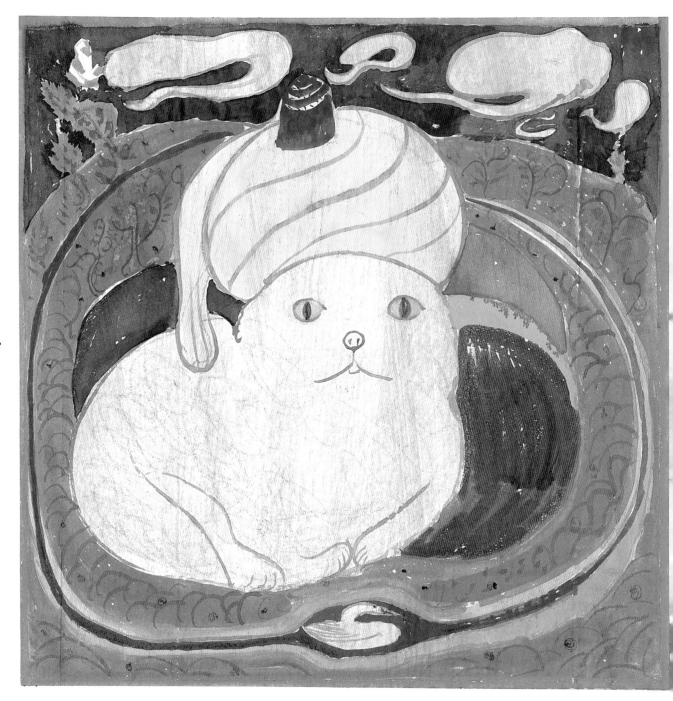

38

The Persian

I am a cat of longhaired version.
A pet-igree that's known as purrrsian.

THE PRAYING MANTIS

Upon a twig
I sit and pray
For something big
To wend my way:
A caterpillar,
Moth,
Or bee—
I swallow them
Religiously.

41

The Coyote

I prowl.
I growl.
My howl
Is throaty.
I love
A vowel,
For I am coyo$^{o^o{}_o}$ote.

The Flounders

Flat as a pancake
Flat as a crepe
Flounders are flat
As a prairie in shape.
While waiting on
Their smooth white side
Below the sand
For food they hide,
Awaiting shrimp
And smaller fishes,
These flattish, mattish
Living dishes.

The Porcupine

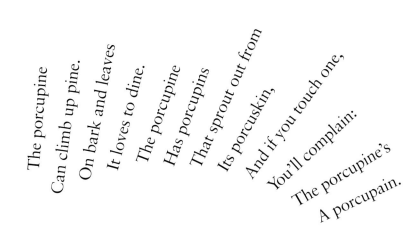

The porcupine
Can climb up pine.
On bark and leaves
It loves to dine.
The porcupine
Has porcupins
That sprout out from
Its porcuskin,
And if you touch one,
You'll complain:
The porcupine's
A porcupain.

THE DADDY LONGLEGS

O Daddy
Daddy O
How'd you get
Those legs to grow
So very long
And lean in size?
From spiderobic
Exercise?
Did you drink milk?
Or chew on cheese?
And by the way,
Where are your knees?
O Daddy
Daddy O
How'd you get
Those legs to grow?

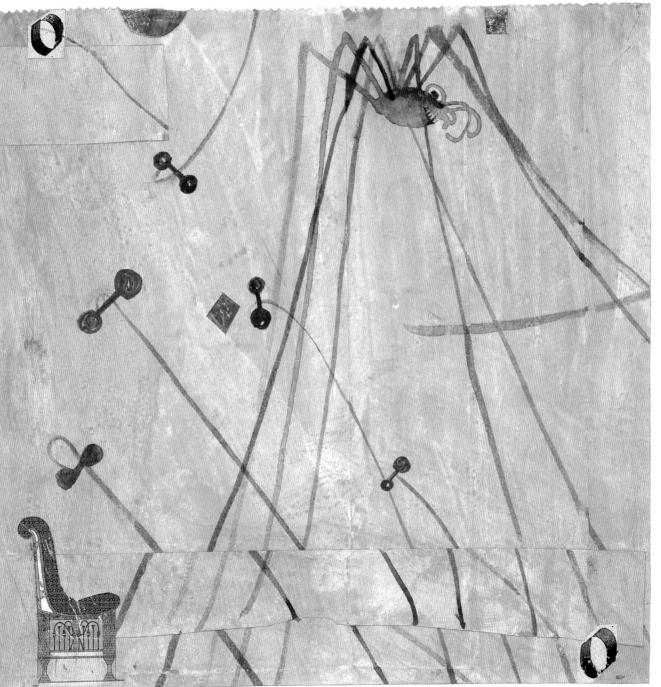

49

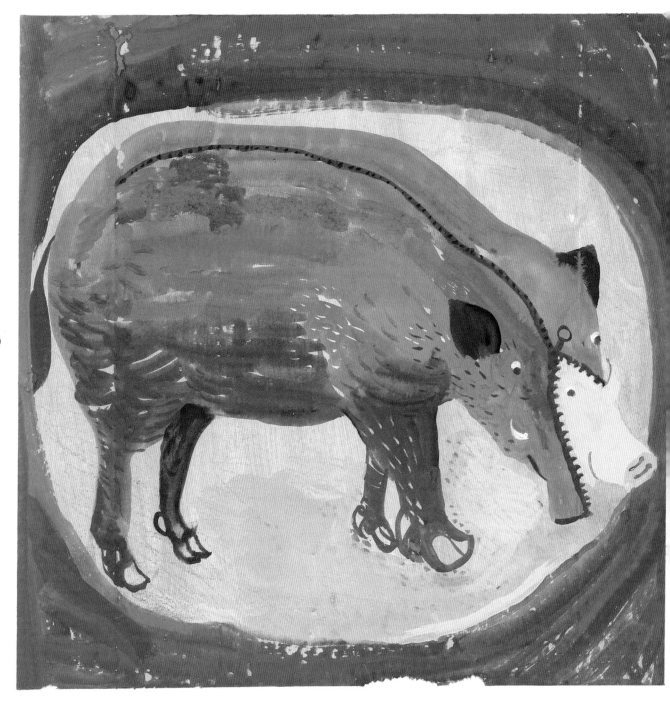

The Boar

The boar at best
Is just a pig
That wears a vest,
And coat, and wig.

The Chihuahua

Chihuahua seems a sorry sight:
So small in stature, weight, and height.
But it can bark a brouhaha:
¡Chi-hua! ¡hua! ¡hua! ¡hua! ¡hua! ¡hua! ¡hua!

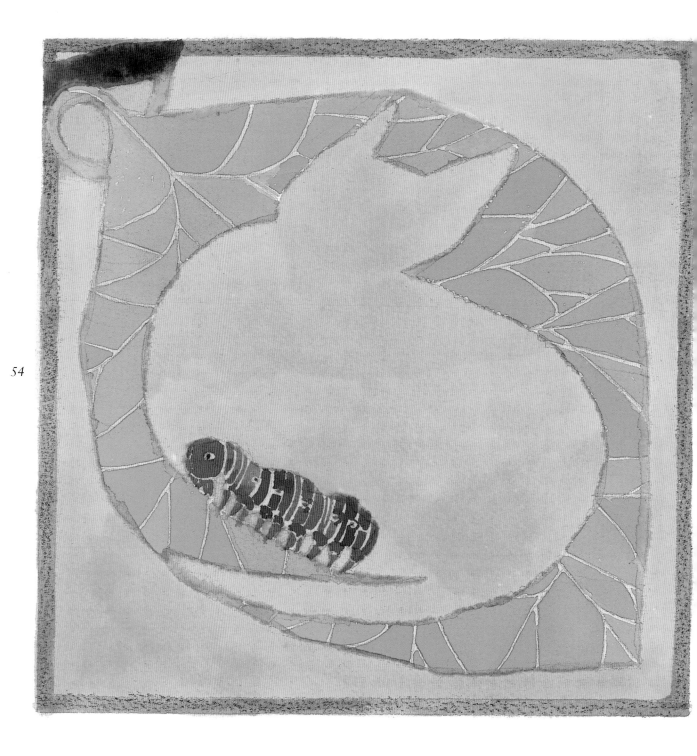

The Caterpillar

The caterpillar's not a cat.
It's very small
And short and fat,
And with those beady little eyes
Will never win a beauty prize.
The caterpillar's brain is small—
It only knows to eat and crawl.
But for this creepy bug don't cry,
It soon will be a butterfly.

The Hawk

I stare
       I glare
I gaze
       I gawk
With keen
Mean eyes
I am the hawk.
All day I pray
For prey to view.
Be thankful if
I don't
See
YOU!

The Cheetah

The cheetah is *fleet*.
The cheetah is *fast*.
Its four furry feet
Have already passed.

The Toad

The tubby toad's so squat and plump
That rarely does it even jump.
At night it feeds on worms and slugs,
Small spiders and assorted bugs,
Then hops into an earthy burrow
To dream of catching more tomorrow.

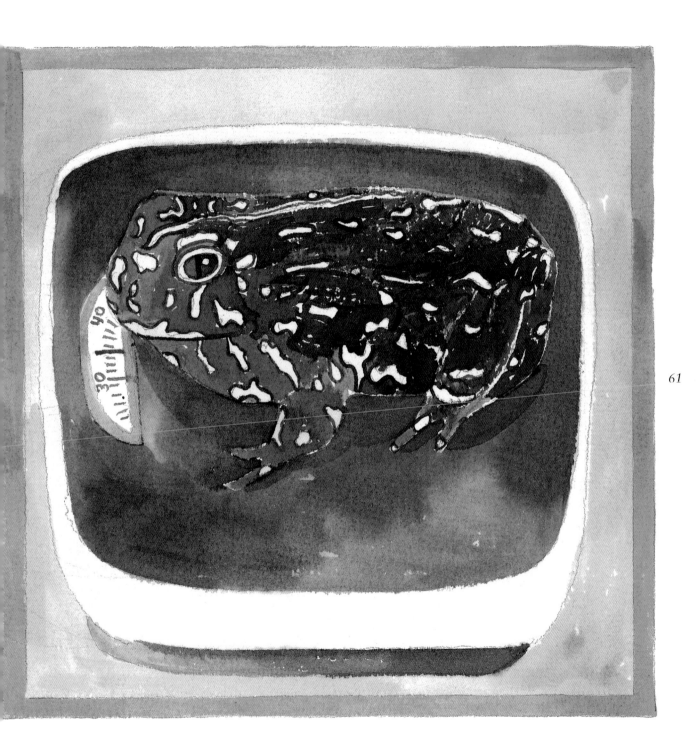

The Walrus

The pounding spatter
Of salty sea
Makes the walrus
Walrusty.

THE CRICKETS

You don't need tickets
To listen to crickets.
They chirp and cheep for free.
They fiddle and sing
By rubbing each wing,
And never will charge you a fee.

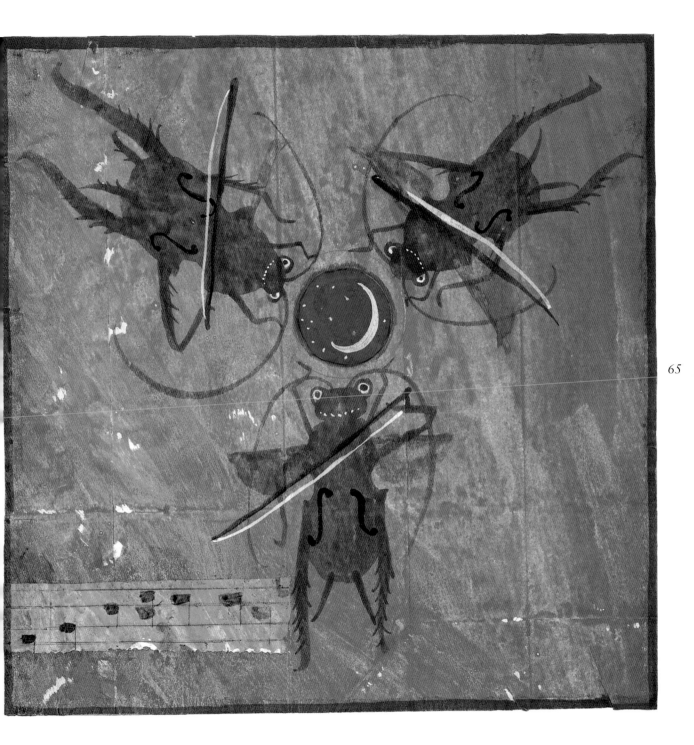

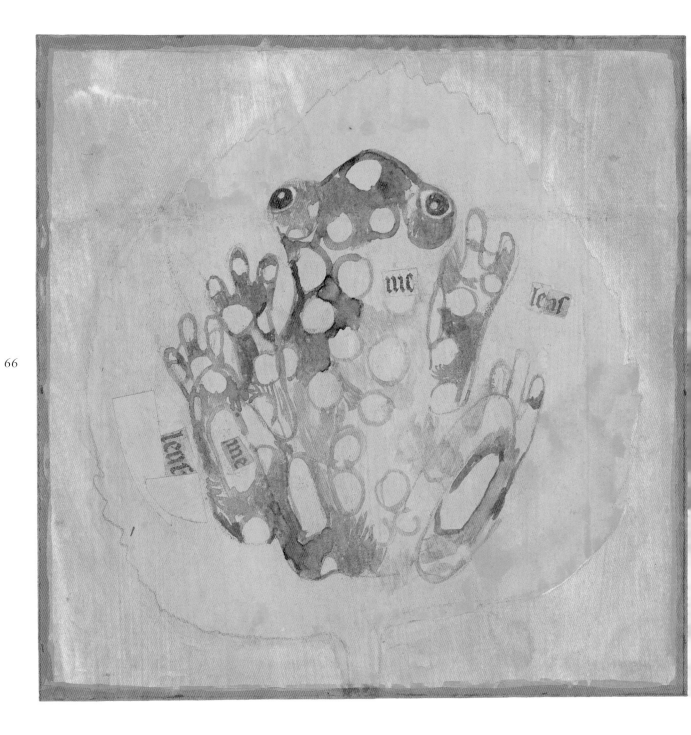

The Glass Frog

Upon a tree
It's hard to see
Which part is leaf
And which is me
Which part is me
And which is leaf
I've lost myself again—
Good grief!

THE MONARCH BUTTERFLY

He is a monarch.
He is a king.
He flies great migrations.
Past nations he wings.
He is a monarch.
He is a prince.
When blackbirds attack him,
From poison they wince.
He is a monarch.
He is a duke.
Swallows that swallow him
Frequently puke.

The Kangaroo

The kangaroo loves to leap.
Into the air it zooms,
While baby's fast asleep
Inside its kangaroom.

The Mule

Voice of the mule: bray
Hue of the mule: bay
Fuel of the mule: hay
Rule of the mule: stay

73

The Newt

Orange nose.
Orange toes.
Orange chin.
Orange skin.
Orange tail.
Orange newt.
Orange you cute
In your bright orange suit.

The Nightjar

By day this bird
Will stay at rest,
For darkness seems
To suit it best,
To chase down insects
Near and far,
And capture night
Inside a jar.

The Bullfrog

Polli-wogger,
Bobby-bogger.
Billy-bellow,
Mellow-fellow.
Hedda-hopper,
Freddy-flopper.
Jimmy-swimmy,
Timmy-shimmy.
Sammy-summer,
Jug-o'-rummer,
Jug-o'-rummer.

The Ocelot

Why ocelots have lots of spots puzzles ocelot.

The Bullfrog

Polli-wogger,
Bobby-bogger.
Billy-bellow,
Mellow-fellow.
Hedda-hopper,
Freddy-flopper.
Jimmy-swimmy,
Timmy-shimmy.
Sammy-summer,
Jug-o'-rummer,
Jug-o'-rummer.

81

Could do with legs!
Just think what we
Our pearly eggs.
Upstream we spawn
We somersault!
We vault!
We jump!
Our leaps astound!
We bound!
We spring!

The Salmon

The Roadrunner

The roadrunner darts
Down dusty roads
In search of insects,
Lizards and toads.
Past tumbleweeds
It *speeds* for snakes,
And catching them,
Turns on the brakes.

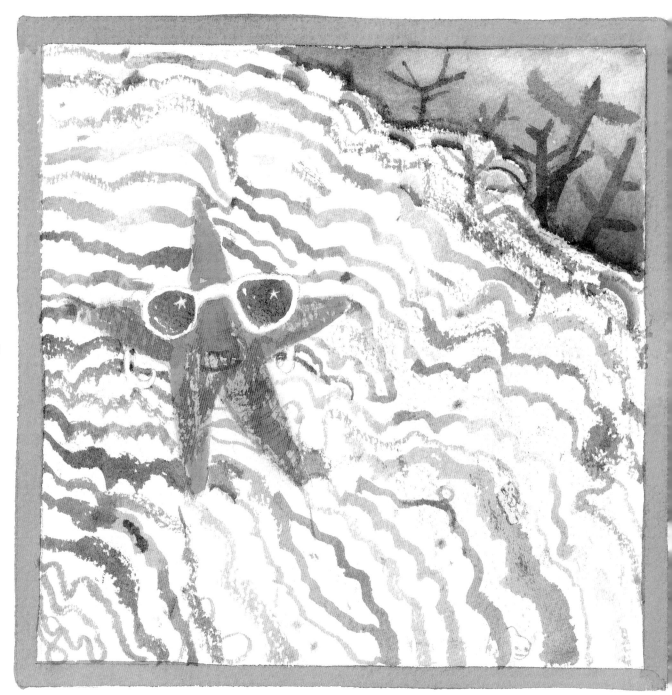

The Starfish

Although it seems
That I'm all arms,
Some other organs
Give me charm.
I have a mouth
With which to feed.
A tiny stomach
Is all I need.
And though it's true
I have no brain,
I'm still a *star*—
I can't complain.

The Python

With thirty feet to squeeze your prey, Python, you take my breath away!

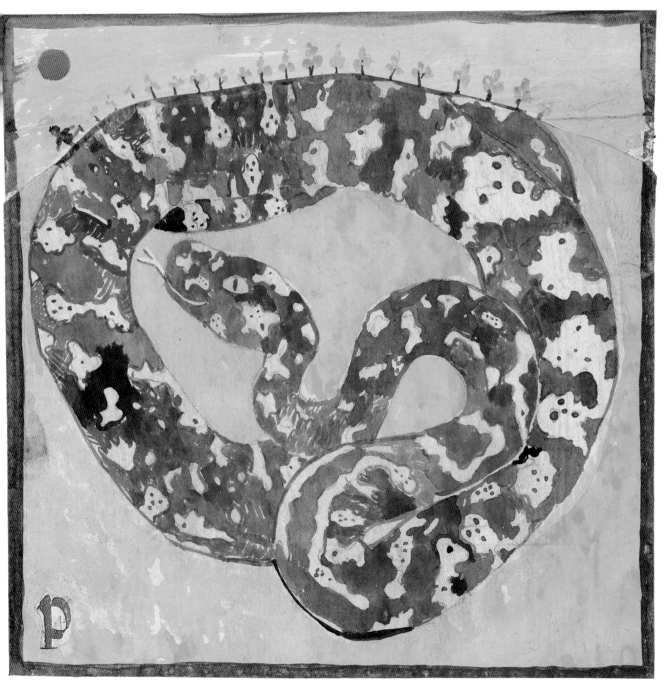

The Woodpeckers

Woodpeckers are *peckuliar* things.
They pick to peck but not to sing.
They rap
   and tap
      for sap in trees
Till some they drum
Look like Swiss cheese.
They thump on stumps of rotting wood
To gobble insects—
Mmmmmmmmmm, tastes good!

The Spring Peepers

Peep,
>   *Peep—*
We steal your sleep.
In scores
>   Of choruses
>   We cheep.
Beneath our chin's
A thin balloon
To help our song
From March till June.
Each spring
>   We sing
>   To bring
A mate,
And make you stay
Awake too late.

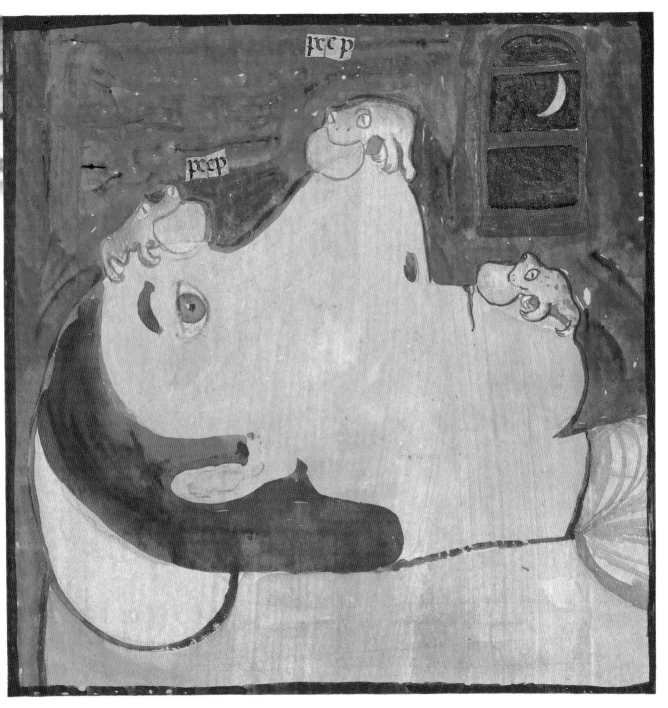

93

94

THE MAYFLY

A mayfly flies
In May or June.
Its life is over
Far too soon.
A day or two
To dance,
To fly—
Hello
Hello
Good-bye
Good-bye.

On the prowl for more?

Dig up Douglas Florian's original creature-poetry collections, where you'll find all the poems in this book—along with many other rollicking animal rhymes.